BURN THE OUTER CORNERS OF THIS PAGE

FLY THIS PAGE

KICK THE BOOK AS FAR AS YOU CAN

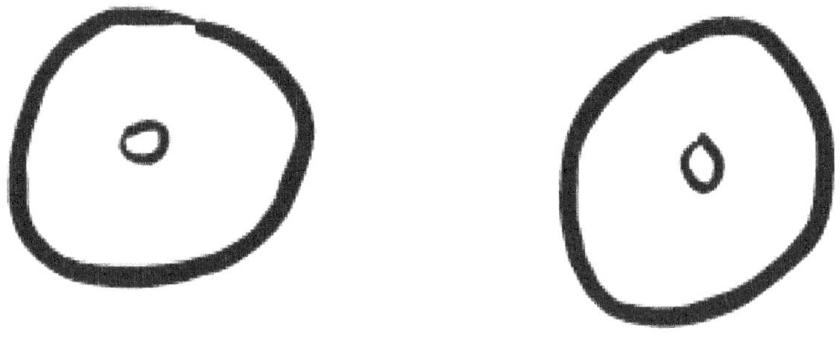

MAKE ME
WATCH A
ROMCOM

CRACK MY SPINE

PERFUME ME

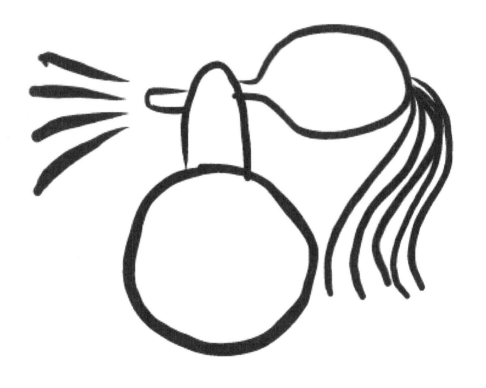

PASTE

HAIR

HERE

BITE THIS
PAGE OFF

PLAY DRUMS WITH COLOR PENCILS

HAND PAINT

HAND PAINT

DRY LEAVES

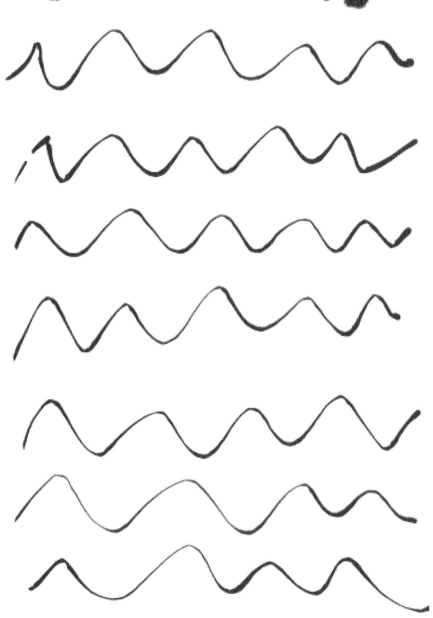

DRY BUGS

LICK THIS
PAGE AFTER
EATING CANDY

DRILL HOLES IN THIS PAGE

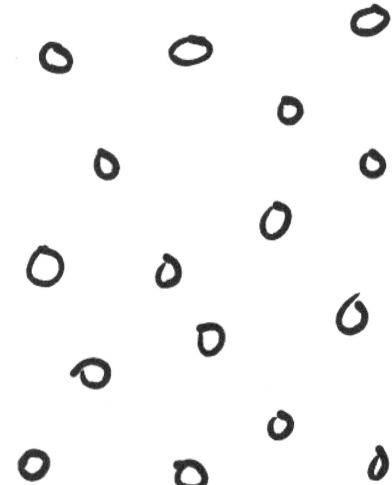

MAKE A COLLAGE

PAINT FEET ART

PAINT FEET ART

DRAW A PLAN OF YOUR HOUSE

FILL THIS PAGE WITH MONSTERS

BLACKEN THIS PAGE

STICK ME
TO THE
OPPOSITE
PAGE

PASTE PEOPLE
FACES HERE

DRAW HERE YOUR DEEPEST DESIRES

WATER COLOR DRAW

DRAW YOUR WORST ENEMY HERE

STRIP THIS
PAGE

BLACK LIST OF PEOPLE

STICK CHEWING GUM

PASTE SEA SHELLS & DRAW SEA ANIMALS

WET DUST
PAINT

GEOMETRIC SHAPES

COLORFUL
DRAW

RIP THIS
PAGE OFF
AND FLOAT
IT

THROW ME AGAINST THE WALLS

USE ME
AS A
FRISBEE

Fill this page with hearts and leave pieces of it on your travels

SCRATCH THIS PAGE WITH A SHARP OBJECT

CHEW THIS PAGE

(DON'T

SWALLOW)

VIOLENT DOODLING

ATTACH
THIS 2
PAGES
SOMEHOW

PASTE
GRASS
HERE

PASTE
GRASS
HERE

MOUTH PAINT MASTERPIECE

Paste face photos and paint facial hair to them

Draw a perfect circle

Paint me and use me to wrap a present

SEW SOMETHING TO ME

SIT
ON ME

STAPLE
ME

Write a poem about
destruction and chaos

Express your feelings
without using words

Express your feelings
with words

DRAW YOUR FACE

Fill this page with the number 6

MAKE THESE PAGES A LIVING SEA

COMPASS DRAWING

MAKE A
BIG HOLE IN
THIS PAGE

Hold the pencils still and move the book to draw

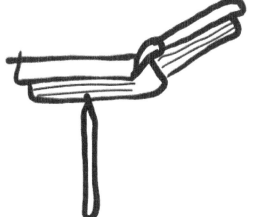

"GET ME
ON THE
FREEZER
FOR 1
DAY" ❄

WALK ME AROUND

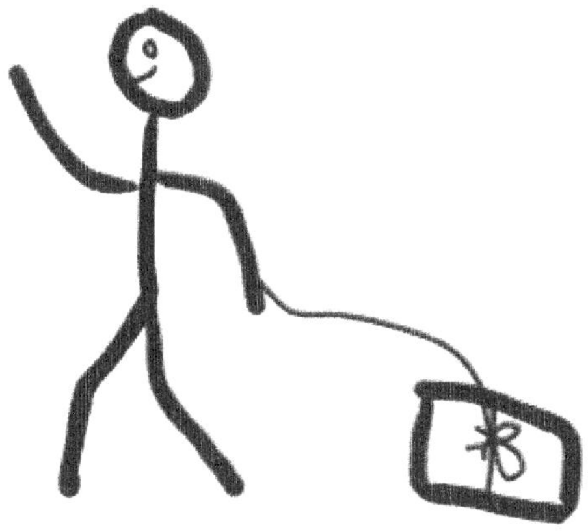

STOMP
ON ME

COLOR ME

MAKE ME
CONFETTI

WHIP ME

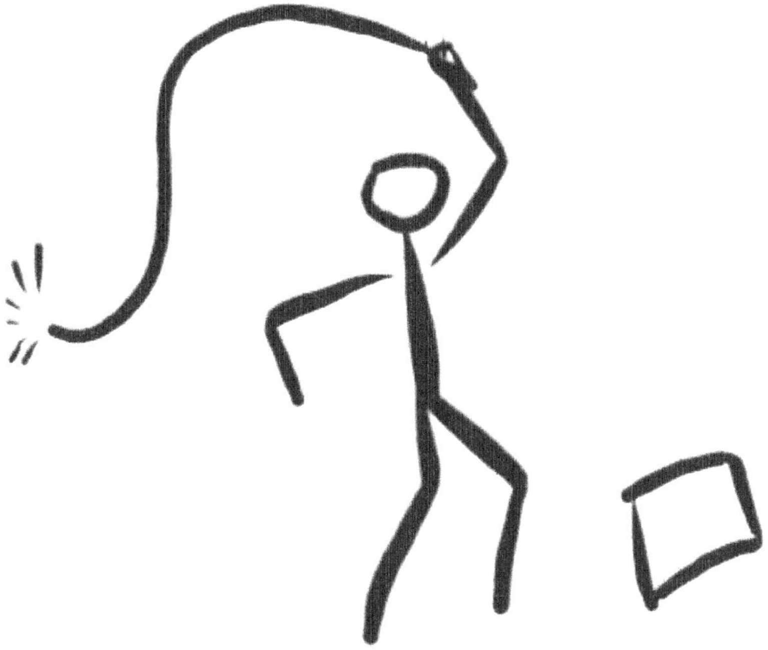

Fs
GO
HERE

PASTE
FEATHERS
HERE

PASTE A RIBBON HERE

PASTE A LITTLE TIE HERE

DESIGN A GRAVE

DRAW A
MIRROR

HIT ME WITH A HAMMER

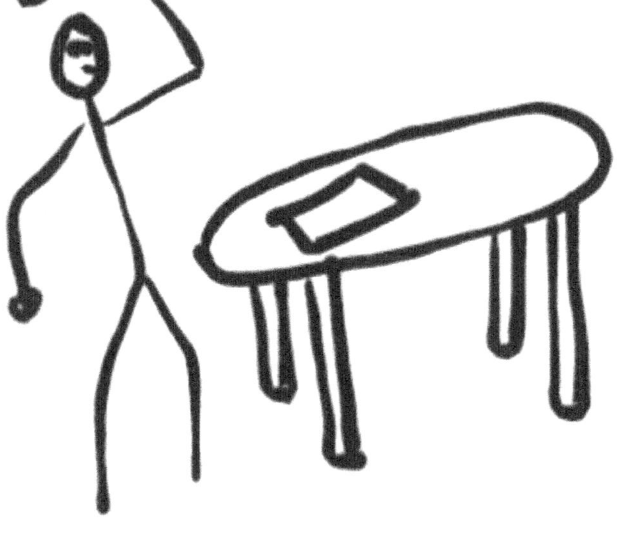

Throw me off a cliff

Bury me for 1 day

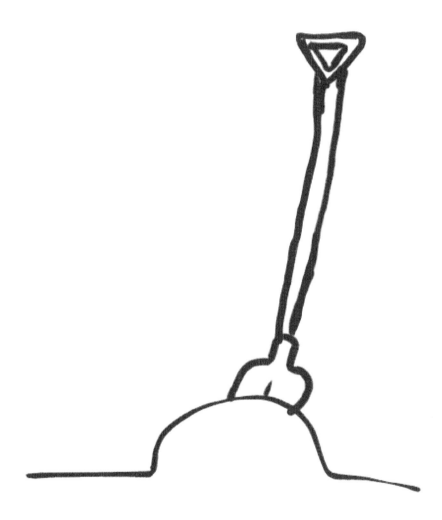

Use me as a footrest

Wrap this page with scotch tape

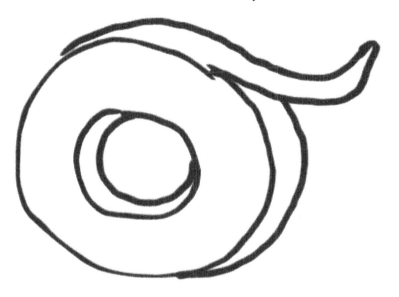

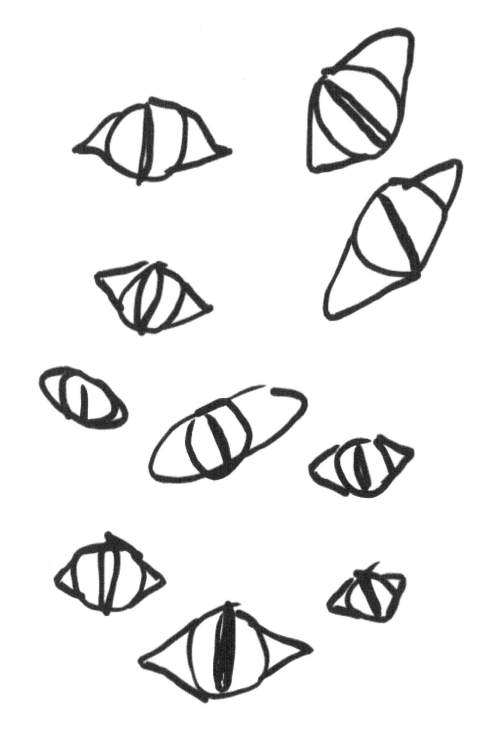

Clean a dirty car window with this page

Stamps go here

STICKERS
GO HERE

DRAW WITH
INK

Draw with detergent

Talcum powder me

COMPOSE
A SONG HERE

Put me in a bag and
sleep with me once.
Then never again.

SPIDERWEBS
HERE

Throw a coin 50 times and write down the results

Draw a bird and a cage with crayons

Make a skull with modelling clay

Bring me to the beach on a sunny day and bury me on the sand

Fill this page with a pencil and draw with an eraser

CHALK
DRAW

Use me as cup holder

SPLASH
A MOSQUITO

SPLASH
A MOSQUITO

Draw with candle wax

Finger prints go here

GIFT
ME TO A
FRIEND

Made in the USA
Monee, IL
23 March 2020